MASTERBUILT

year
XXX

20
17

STEPHEN PITKIN

Hal Leonard Books / an imprint of Hal Leonard LLC

Copyright © 2017 Hal Leonard LLC

All rights reserved. No part of this book may be reproduced in any form or by any electronic or mechanical means including information storage and retrieval systems without permission in writing from the publisher, except by a reviewer, who may quote brief passages in a review.

Published in 2017 by Hal Leonard Books
An Imprint of Hal Leonard LLC
7777 W. Bluemound Road
Milwaukee, WI 53213

Trade Book Division Editorial Offices
33 Plymouth St., Montclair, NJ 07042

Printed in China

Book Design by Pitkin Studio

Library of Congress Cataloging-in-Publication Data
is available upon request

ISBN: 978-1-4950-7391-5

First Edition

All photography, narration and design created by Pitkin Studio.

MASTER BUILT YEAR XXX CONTENTS

MASTER BUILT MOJO INFUSED **THE PHOTOS** STEPHEN PITKIN	4
MASTER BUILT MOJO INFUSED **THE MUSIC** BILLY GIBBONS	6
MASTER BUILT MOJO INFUSED **THE GUITARS** MIKE LEWIS	8
MOJO MAKERS **THE TEAM 1999** STEPHEN PITKIN	10
MOJO MAKERS **THE TEAM 2016** STEPHEN PITKIN	11
THE **GUITARS** STEPHEN PITKIN	12
ACKNOWLEDGMENTS	160

MASTER BUILT MOJO INFUSED THE PHOTOS

Since 1995 I have been privileged to explore, observe and photograph incredible things in the people and guitars of the Fender Custom Shop. I am excited to share some of the discoveries I have made with you through the images that fill the pages of this book.

The masterbuilders and apprentices are true mojo makers, building each guitar with astonishing levels of skill and innovation, infusing elements of their personal creativity into the instruments they build. Leo Fender's time honored traditions are held to the highest standard by the builders while collaborating with artists and musicians who rely on these custom instruments for the music they create.

This is a book where detailed photographs illustrate the instruments and personal stories share the inspiration and passion behind the extraordinary achievements in craftsmanship and creativity. Stories are told in the words of artists and builders with the intent of immersing you into the creative process and the culture of the Fender Custom Shop.

I hope every page of this book is a window of discovery for you, inspiring curiosity and encouraging your imagination to dream of a masterpiece when it is in your hands.

Stephen Pitkin

Great photography has everything to do with making a captivating image and engaging others in a shared moment of discovery.

Stephen Pitkin, 2016

"Crossroads" Limited Edition Stratocaster® / 2007, Work in process at Pitkin Studio

MASTER BUILT MOJO INFUSED THE MUSIC

From the outset, the visual impact of Fender's modern styling created an almost instant appeal with the unexpected first foray into fabrication of Leo's vision of a Spanish electric 6-string guitar. In fast fashion, the curiously magnetic draw of this somewhat new entry into the field brought some fearless followers around willing to *"kick the tires"* and take 'er for a spin around the block and see what the invitation to *"give it a try"* might offer.

With this exciting introduction came the accompaniment of Leo's acknowledgment of the value of image alongside the business of function and utility. And here, through the work behind the lens, is Steve Pitkin's continuing photographic presentation, which stands steadfastly in line with the fine Fender tradition of showcasing the beauty of guitar design which has remained an important element of admiration from the earliest beginnings through the present.

Mr. Pitkin is certainly no stranger to the call for excellence upholding Fender's demand for quality. For over 25 years, now at the time of this publication, Steve has masterfully captured angle after angle of the many instruments in the wide range of models the factory rolls off the assembly line, and moreover, Steve zero's in on the paramount importance of Fender's *"Custom Shop"* creations as well. Going back to the beginnings, Steve has constantly maintained an acute awareness of Leo Fender's painstaking production plans, which ultimately forged a worldly embrace and perception of simplicity-meets-electricity.

The guitar side of Steve's penchant and prowess with his trusty array of all-things-camera, especially attention to high resolution detail, goes back to his early days banging on guitar. No wonder the works included on these pages take in everything. Across the board, there are superb views spotlighting Fender's rare, Bass VI and Double-necks, to highlighting the recent introduction of the exotic, vintage styled, *"El Cabron"*.

Nothing is left to chance to insure enjoyment for those with appreciation of checking out the Custom Shop's best-of-the-best and Fender's baddest of the bad…!
Go ahead, turn up the volume and flip through the pages for a genuine flip and trip.

Rock on!

Billy Gibbons

My discussion with Keith Richards about the creative process led me to believe there's an invisible presence, a stream of ever-flowing creativity that we overhear.

All you have to do is pull up the antenna and dial it in. This presence allows you to maintain your sense of origin, re-member the pieces, cut, shuffle and move forward.

Billy Gibbons, 2016

The Reverend Billy Gibbons preachin' the gospel of guitar with *"El Cabron"*

MASTER BUILT MOJO INFUSED THE GUITARS

The origins of the Custom Shop can be traced back to the early days of Leo Fender. Leo loved music and musicians. He loved hanging out with musicians and he built many custom instruments for working artists right from the beginning. When you walk through the halls of this factory you will see photographs of Leo with various artists visiting the shop trying out equipment, he would lend out guitars and amps to be tested and listened to what artists wanted in their instruments. There is evidence that many custom instruments were made for artists with unique colors and other specialized features.

From the beginning Leo Fender focused on the core needs of working artists. What mattered most to him was making the best possible tools for musicians and being the inventor he was, never followed the lead of others. He created his own way of making instruments that we continue to push forward to this day. The Leo Fender Ethos is in the grain of the Custom Shop where we live by the mantra that *every one you make is the best you've ever made*. We continue improving and refuse to peak out.

When it comes to a great guitar, it's not just about the design or the specs. As with fine food, it's about the ingredients, the way they are prepared, the tools that are used and the people who make it. We have people that have been here since 1960, working every day, making parts, sanding necks and building instruments that have ended up in the hands of some of our most beloved artists, songwriters and performers. All that is built into everything we make and when I say, *mojo included*, that's exactly what I mean.

Mike Lewis

This tool was mounted on its shoes in 1959 when Fender was prototyping the Jazz Bass. It's the tool that made the very first bridge cover and same tool that will be making them tomorrow. Every single one has been made on this tool. Think about all the instruments these parts were built into, the hands they ended up in, the music that was written, played and recorded on them, music that is now woven into the fabric of our culture.

Mike Lewis, 2016

Jazz Bass® bridge cover stamping tool / 1959

MOJO MAKERS THE TEAM / 2016

RHINESTONE STRATOCASTER FRED STUART

RHINESTONE STRATOCASTER DETAIL FRED STUART

CUSTOM JAG-STANG LARRY BROOKS

CUSTOM JAG-STANG DETAIL LARRY BROOKS

CUSTOM JAZZ BASS JW BLACK

CUSTOM JAZZ BASS DETAIL JW BLACK

WORKBENCH DETAILS FRED STUART

FIRST RELIC STRATOCASTER JW BLACK

FIRST RELIC STRATOCASTER DETAIL JW BLACK

BIRD OF FIRE STRATOCASTER JOHN PAGE

MONTEREY POP FESTIVAL STRATOCASTER PAMELINA H

MONTEREY POP FESTIVAL STRATOCASTER DETAIL PAMELINA H

INSTALLING A BRIDGE ALAN HAMEL

CARL PERKINS CUSTOM TELECASTER ALAN HAMEL

CUSTOM DELUXE ARCHTOP STEPHEN STERN

CARVING AN ULTRA TOP STEPHEN STERN

MUDDY WATERS TRIBUTE TELECASTER JOHN CRUZ

CATALINA BLUES FESTIVAL STRATOCASTER PAMELINA H

THE GUITARS

CATALINA BLUES FESTIVAL DETAIL STRATOCASTER PAMELINA H

SKELETELE TELECASTER CHRIS FLEMING

SURFBOARD STRATOCASTER DENNIS GALUSZKA

SURFBOARD STRATOCASTER DETAIL DENNIS GALUSZKA

SRV NUMBER ONE STRATOCASTER JOHN CRUZ

BURNISHING ELECTRONICS SHIELDING JOHN CRUZ

GEORGE WASHINGTON CUSTOM ESQUIRE MIKE ELDRED

TROY LEE DESIGNS STRATOCASTER TODD KRAUSE

EL CABRON CHRIS FLEMING

EL CABRON DETAIL CHRIS FLEMING

SANDING A NECK JOINT JOHN ENGLISH

ROSEWOOD NECK PROTOTYPE JOHN ENGLISH

ROSEWOOD NECK PROTOTYPE DETAIL JOHN ENGLISH

BUDDY GUY CUSTOM TELECASTER YURIY SHISHKOV

BUDDY GUY CUSTOM TELECASTER DETAIL YURIY SHISHKOV

JEFF BECK TRIBUTE TELECASTER JOHN CRUZ

JEFF BECK TRIBUTE TELECASTER DETAIL JOHN CRUZ

MASTER SALUTE STRATOCASTER MARK KENDRICK

SPLATOCASTER STRATOCASTER SCOTT BUEHL

SPLATOCASTER STRATOCASTER DETAIL SCOTT BUEHL

BLACKIE TRIBUTE STRATOCASTER TODD KRAUSE

MOJO MAKERS ABBY AND GEORGE

CUSTOM STRATOCASTER JASON SMITH

CUSTOM STRATOCASTER DETAIL JASON SMITH

KOICASTER STRATOCASTER TODD KRAUSE

KOICASTER STRATOCASTER DETAIL TODD KRAUSE

JAZZMASTER BASS VI DOUBLENECK DENNIS GALUSZKA

PRE-CUTTING A NUT DENNIS GALUSZKA

DAVE NEWMAN TELECASTER GREG FESSLER

DAVE NEWMAN TELECASTER DETAIL GREG FESSLER

BIRDFLOWER TELECASTER YURIY SHISHKOV

BIRDFLOWER TELECASTER DETAIL YURIY SHISHKOV

SPARKLE FLAME STRATOCASTER DENNIS GALUSZKA

LIBERTY STRATOCASTER DALE WILSON

RASCAL BASS JASON SMITH

RASCAL BASS DETAIL JASON SMITH

THE GUITARS

CHECKING NECK BOW JASON SMITH

CARVED TOP TELECASTER PAUL WALLER

CARVED TOP TELECASTER DETAIL PAUL WALLER

HERMITAGE STRATOCASTER YURIY SHISHKOV

HERMITAGE STRATOCASTER DETAIL YURIY SHISHKOV

SUNSET QUILT MAPLE STRATOCASTER PAUL WALLER

MASTODON BASS VI DENNIS GALUSZKA

MASTODON BASS VI DETAIL DENNIS GALUSZKA

SANDING FRETBOARD ROLL DENNIS GALUSZKA

CUSTOM PRECISION BASS GREG FESSLER

JAWBREAKER STRATOCASTER DALE WILSON

JAWBREAKER STRATOCASTER DETAIL DALE WILSON

PROFILING A NUT DALE WILSON

STAINED GLASS TELECASTER DALE WILSON

CARDBOARD STRATOCASTER PAUL WALLER

ROSEWOOD FLAME MAPLE STRATOCASTER GREG FESSLER

ROSEWOOD FLAME MAPLE STRATOCASTER DETAIL GREG FESSLER

STRATOCASTER DESIGN INSPIRATION GEORGE FULLERTON

Rhinestone Stratocaster® / 1993, Masterbuilder, Fred Stuart

I remember specifically my friend Pam and I visiting the Liberace Museum in Las Vegas. Liberace had this white piano covered in rhinestones at the museum and I just realized we could really do some interesting things with rhinestones on a guitar. I went into the LA garment district and they had a couple shops there that sell nothing but rhinestones so we had quite a selection to draw from. I thought the rhinestones would be great for a grape and vine motif. George Amicay and I put our heads together on how to build this guitar. It's made with Corian® over an ash body and maple neck. George carved the design, set the jewels and covered the vines in gold.

We had done several art guitars prior to this one but this project seemed to push everything over the top. At the time, this guitar stretched the limits of what had been done. It was right in that era when we were all starting to stretch out a little bit and do some pretty cool things. I guess it's fair to say this guitar was a quantum leap from what we had done with art guitars before that time. I've always said that if Liberace played guitar this one would have been his.

Fred Stuart, 2016

Rhinestone Stratocaster® / 1993, Masterbuilder, Fred Stuart

In 1993, I was working in R&D. After finishing up with Stu Hamm and in the midst of bass drawings for Roscoe Beck, Larry brought over this pieced together Polaroid photo construction he just received from Kurt. I had some Jazzmaster templates at my bench and the lines were very similar. Larry had made Mustang templates, as we didn't have them at that time. He asked if I'd help him make the drawings and some of the prototype templates based upon the photo comp.
Kurt had taken Polaroid photos of his Jaguar and his Mustang, cut the two photos in half and taped them together. It was really rough but we got the idea. He then used whiteout correction fluid to cover the misaligned parts and drew in the missing pieces with a ballpoint pen.

Kurt wanted to build this hybrid guitar, something really unique. Nirvana was at that time on top of the mountain, pop or heavy metal. the alternative music movement seemed to overtake most everything else.

Nirvana had become a phenom and we were making the stuff Kurt was playing. Other guitar companies scrambled to emulate something like this with moto pickguards and vintage style guitar designs. Fender was doing this stuff all along; nothing had to change here because we had the guitar building roots that all the others were trying to tap into. After all was said and done, I believe Larry built four of these custom Jag-Stangs for Kurt.

Mark Kendrick, 2016

Custom Jag-Stang / 1993, Masterbuilder, Larry Brooks

Custom Jag-Stang / 1993, Masterbuilder, Larry Brooks

Custom Jazz Bass® / 1994, Masterbuilder, Jay W. Black

We wanted to show these basses as a Fender Custom Shop version of what was happening in the boutique marketplace at that time. Basses were not a common item for us to build in the Custom Shop. This Jazz Bass was one of a matched set, paired with a five-string partner and both basses were made with matching quilt maple tops on ash bodies. Hence, the fancy wood, abalone block inlay and neck binding. These basses were built with EMG pick-ups and fitted with a custom pre-amp built by John Suhr. This type of instrument is more common now, but not the norm in those days for the Custom Shop.

They were constructed in April, of 1994 for the Summer NAMM Show in Nashville, then went on tour around the world to our special dealers as part of a Custom Shop road tour, promoting some of our best work.

Jay W. Black, 2016

Custom Jazz Bass® / 1994, Masterbuilder, Jay W. Black

Workbench details / 1995, Masterbuilder, Fred Stuart

Here it is, the Flotsam and Jetsam of a guitar builders bench. The pick-up at the bottom is a Jazzmaster, there is a chunk of the Velvet Elvis roping which I was working on at the time, guitar picks, frets and nuts, decals, herringbone purfling and even my calipers that served as the perfect Crescent wrench when in a pinch.

Fred Stuart, 2016

First Relic Stratocaster® / 1995, Masterbuilder, Jay W. Black

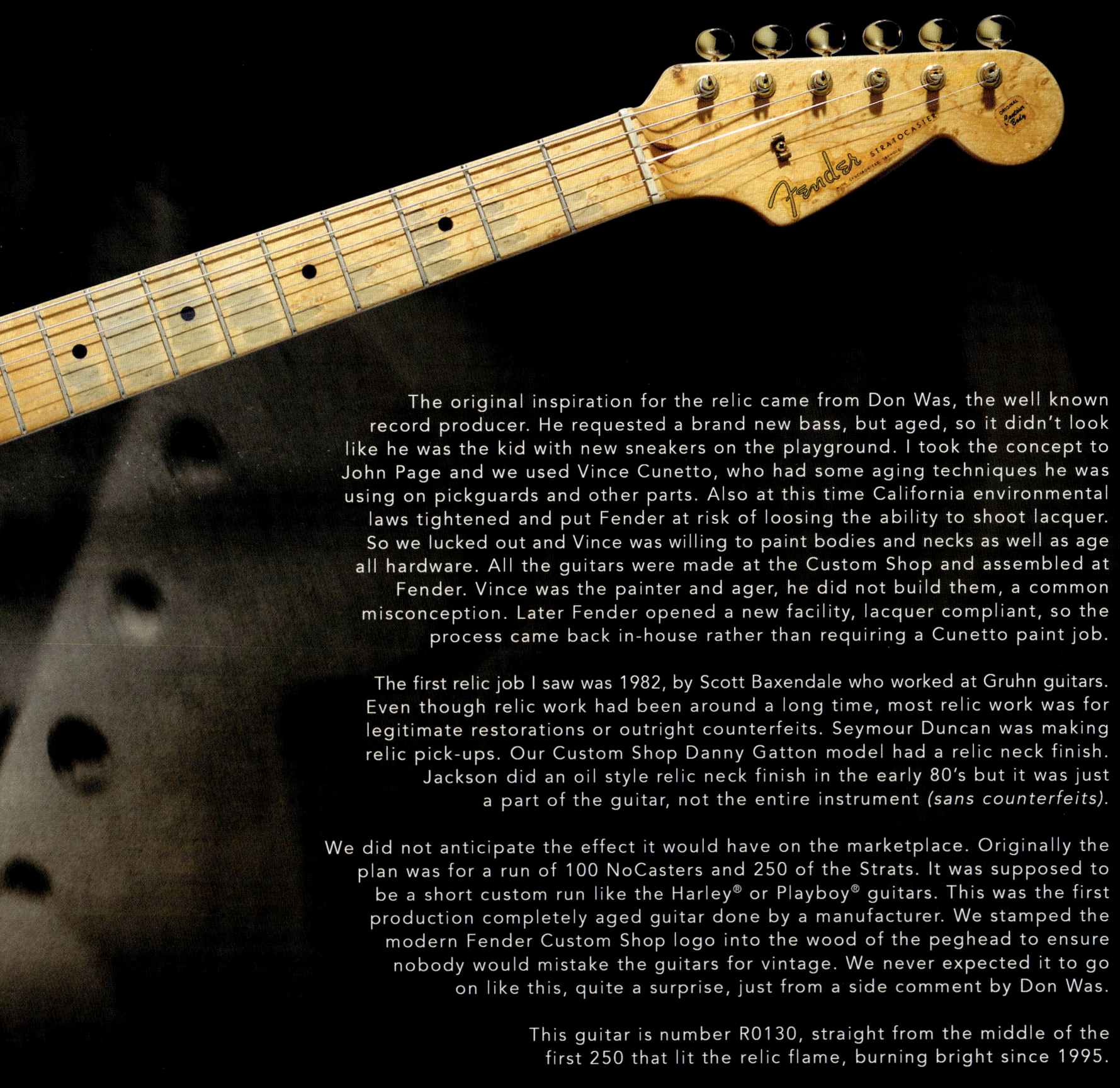

The original inspiration for the relic came from Don Was, the well known record producer. He requested a brand new bass, but aged, so it didn't look like he was the kid with new sneakers on the playground. I took the concept to John Page and we used Vince Cunetto, who had some aging techniques he was using on pickguards and other parts. Also at this time California environmental laws tightened and put Fender at risk of loosing the ability to shoot lacquer. So we lucked out and Vince was willing to paint bodies and necks as well as age all hardware. All the guitars were made at the Custom Shop and assembled at Fender. Vince was the painter and ager, he did not build them, a common misconception. Later Fender opened a new facility, lacquer compliant, so the process came back in-house rather than requiring a Cunetto paint job.

The first relic job I saw was 1982, by Scott Baxendale who worked at Gruhn guitars. Even though relic work had been around a long time, most relic work was for legitimate restorations or outright counterfeits. Seymour Duncan was making relic pick-ups. Our Custom Shop Danny Gatton model had a relic neck finish. Jackson did an oil style relic neck finish in the early 80's but it was just a part of the guitar, not the entire instrument *(sans counterfeits)*.

We did not anticipate the effect it would have on the marketplace. Originally the plan was for a run of 100 NoCasters and 250 of the Strats. It was supposed to be a short custom run like the Harley® or Playboy® guitars. This was the first production completely aged guitar done by a manufacturer. We stamped the modern Fender Custom Shop logo into the wood of the peghead to ensure nobody would mistake the guitars for vintage. We never expected it to go on like this, quite a surprise, just from a side comment by Don Was.

This guitar is number R0130, straight from the middle of the first 250 that lit the relic flame, burning bright since 1995.

Jay W. Black, 2016

First Relic Stratocaster® / 1995, Masterbuilder Jay W. Black

"Bird of Fire" Stratocaster® / 1995, John Page

In my effort to always push the envelope with art guitars, we created the *Bird of Fire* Stratocaster. I was inspired by the old movie *Metropolis*, one of my favorite pieces of Deco art is *Oiseau de Feu*, by Rene Lalique, master glass artisan, made in 1925. I was stunned by its beauty and wanted to see how it would translate to a guitar. In addition, as we did quite a bit back then, I wanted to create a new and unique package, an art guitar AND piece of art that could hang on the wall. The final package was the collaborative effort of five artists... Rene Lalique, inspiration from his original work, Pamelina H., conceptual art and original painting, Gene Baker, guitar building, Larry Robinson, inlay, and myself, original concept, direction and picture frame.

The guitar is beautifully crafted from extremely rare quilted Honduran mahogany, and inlayed with multiple varieties of exotic shell, metals and plastics. The original painting puts the *Bird of Fire* in her retro-futuristic Deco perch, and is housed in a handmade, Deco motif frame, made of matching quilted Honduran mahogany, Madagascar ebony and flamed maple. One of my favorite Custom Shop creations!

John Page, 2016

The guitar Jimi Hendrix painted, smashed and burned at the music festival was a fiesta red Stratocaster he had painted specifically for that performance. Jimi partially painted over the red body with white spray paint then applied swirling designs with various colors of model car paint. The custom paint was crudely applied and overspray from the white paint was all over the hardware. He used poor quality brushes to apply the hearts and swirls design so the detail was a bit rough. The decoration of Jimi's guitar was made to go up in flames. Its creation and destruction were all part of his performance. I individually painted 210 of these tribute guitars for the limited edition set.

This guitar was an amazing project to work on and yet we had nothing to work with for reference except a video of Jimi playing at the Monterey Pop Festival. No photographs of the original guitar are known from before it went onstage for the performance. I spent four or five hours watching the video frame by frame, with a sketchbook in hand and drawing over and over again details I could see. From my collection of sketches I made several composite drawings to share with John Page.

We went through seven prototype guitar bodies before settling on a final design for the tribute guitar. We didn't feel obligated to make a perfect copy of what Jimi made to be smashed on stage and we knew the final design was prettier than Jimi's original painting but John asked me to *Pamelina* the design up a bit, he thought it would be an appropriate tribute to Hendrix and the 30th Anniversary of the famed '67 performance.

Pamelina H., 2016

Monterey Pop Festival Tribute Stratocaster / 1999, Fullerton, CA.

Monterey Pop Festival Tribute Stratocaster® / 1997, Pamelina H.

Installing a bridge / 1995, Masterbuilder, Alan Hamel

I got my start as a guitar builder working with Dale Fortune at Fortune Guitars in the mid-70's. I was playing in a band doing some repair work of my own and had painted, sanded and buffed a couple guitar bodies that were ready to be built. I took the finished bodies to Fortune Guitars to see if we could get them to finish the necks and hardware. I pulled the bodies out of the pillowcases and he pretty much offered me a job on the spot. Dale had a pretty serious backlog of guitars that needed finishing at that time.

I painted guitars for about three months then started doing other types of bench work in the shop under his supervision. Soon enough Dale gave me the rope to get started putting entire guitars together and he kept an eye on my work to steer me into a good direction. Mark Kendrick also got his start with Fortune Guitars. Dale was instrumental in getting a whole bunch of us off the ground in the 70's.

I built this guitar the second or third year of my time working in the Custom Shop. At that particular time tribal tattoos were really popular in Southern California. Mike Ponce who worked in the shop had a lot of interesting tattoos and I asked him to help me come up with a design that would work on a Strat. I wanted to create a design that would move from the body into the neck and the pickguard with continuity and gave Mike free reign to do that, build the tribal design into the whole guitar.

Alan Hamel, 2016

Carl Perkins Custom Telecaster® / 1999, Masterbuilder, Alan Hamel

This Carl Perkins guitar was definitely the highlight of all my time working in the Custom Shop. Mike Eldred was playing a gig with Lee Rocker, the bass player from The Stray Cats. They were opening a show for Carl Perkins at the House of Blues in Hollywood. Mike invited me to come along to the show and I was really sorry to see Carl playing a sad looking two pick-up Stratocaster type guitar that looked to be of below average quality. I reached out to Carl back stage and got a message to him asking if I could possibly work with him to build a better quality guitar for him, something that would represent his importance as an artist and the incredible contributions he has made in music.

The follow-up conversations with him were amazing, he was so appreciative of everything we offered and what we finally created for him is this guitar. In talking to Carl. I realized what a down-to-earth humble person he was. We came up with the blue sparkle idea, the blue suede pickguard and the inlaid neck and he was appreciative of all those special design ideas. The one thing he really was hoping for in his new guitar was a Bigsby, like what he used to play in the old days. It took some special effort but we finally got Bigsby to dig out their original casting patterns with the Fender logo cast into the baseplate. I modified the Bigsby by splitting the tension roller so the bass and treble strings could roll independently of each other, pulled the pins and re-drilled the string bar in order to attach the strings which helps the guitar stay in tune. Carl loved this guitar and played it through to the end of his life.

Alan Hamel, 2016

Custom Deluxe® Archtop / 1999, Masterbuilder, Stephen Stern

I wanted to do a 50's style Rockabilly guitar and was working with Jimmy D'Aquisto at the time. I came up with the idea of using vintage DeArmond pick-ups from the 50s'. I was able to get some of Fred Stewart's handmade purfling for the guitar. The paint is a two-tone color combination with blue top and cream colored back and sides, reminiscent of the two-tone car paint jobs of the 50's. For the logo on the peghead I created a Fender Custom Shop chevron, cut and filed out of brass then the Fender F was applied to the top after paint. The neck inlays were modeled after the scaled diamond patterns that I saw used in lap-steels of that era.

Stephen Stern, 2016

In this photo I'm carving the surface of an *Ultra* guitar top. The first step is to rough carve the thickness with a routing machine then plane the inside to bring the thickness into spec. Those first steps are followed-up with scraping and sanding to the final size. Actually the router available at the time was not as accurate as carving the wood by hand. The curved arch-top tapers down in thickness toward the edges then is beefed back up around the rim so the top can act as a drumhead. The top moves as it is played pushing sound waves off the back and then out the sound holes.

The tradition of carved-top guitars allows for lighter bracing altogether creating a more mellow sound typically used in jazz style music. It does take a lot of practice to get this right. As you carve, listen and feel the wood, your senses combine and begin to understand where things are coming into shape.
The only way to really do this right is by using all of your senses as you work
rather than taking measurements along the way.

Stephen Stern, 2016

Ultra top carving / 1995, Masterbuilder, Stephen Stern

Muddy Waters Tribute Telecaster® / 2000, Masterbuilder, John Cruz

This was the first Tribute guitar for the Custom Shop. John Page wanted to do a Limited Edition Tribute rather than a signature model for Muddy Waters and introduce it at the Catalina Blues Festival.

I was the one who went to the Rock-n-Roll Hall of Fame to spec out the guitar. Usually we deal with artist instruments here at the shop and it's no big deal for us to handle, but there you Do Not Touch, you handle every artifact with white gloves only. I realized the strings had been on the guitar since Muddy played it 15 years earlier, they were all rusted and I just panicked that I might break one.

I did some research before I went and found Muddy did not have many guitars, he had this guitar and I believed at the time there were two other Muddy Waters guitars out there, an early '58 blonde Tele and a later red '64 Custom, but it turned out that it was the '58 blonde which had been modified midway through its life. The red guitar I was working with actually WAS the blonde, now repainted and with a different neck *(a '64 Tele Custom)* put on it. He really played just this one guitar in its two different configurations. Those were details we didn't know until I got into the guitar and could study it in pieces.

The Custom Shop had been doing relics for quite awhile, but this was the first to match the specific details of an exact relic guitar. John Cruz did the first one and because he did such a great job with it he ended up doing all of them. This project pushed the envelope to a new place and from there we did the Rory Gallagher, SRV, Blackie and others.

I also went with Mike Eldred to look at the Jimi Hendrix Woodstock Strat up in Seattle and again, they were very reticent about any kind of tools touching it. Mike pointed to me and said, *"He took Muddy Waters' guitar apart at the RRHF,"* which is what it took to let us work on the Hendrix guitar. That was cool because everything seems to begin with Muddy Waters.

George Blanda, 2016

Catalina Blues Festival Stratocaster® / 2001, Pamelina H.

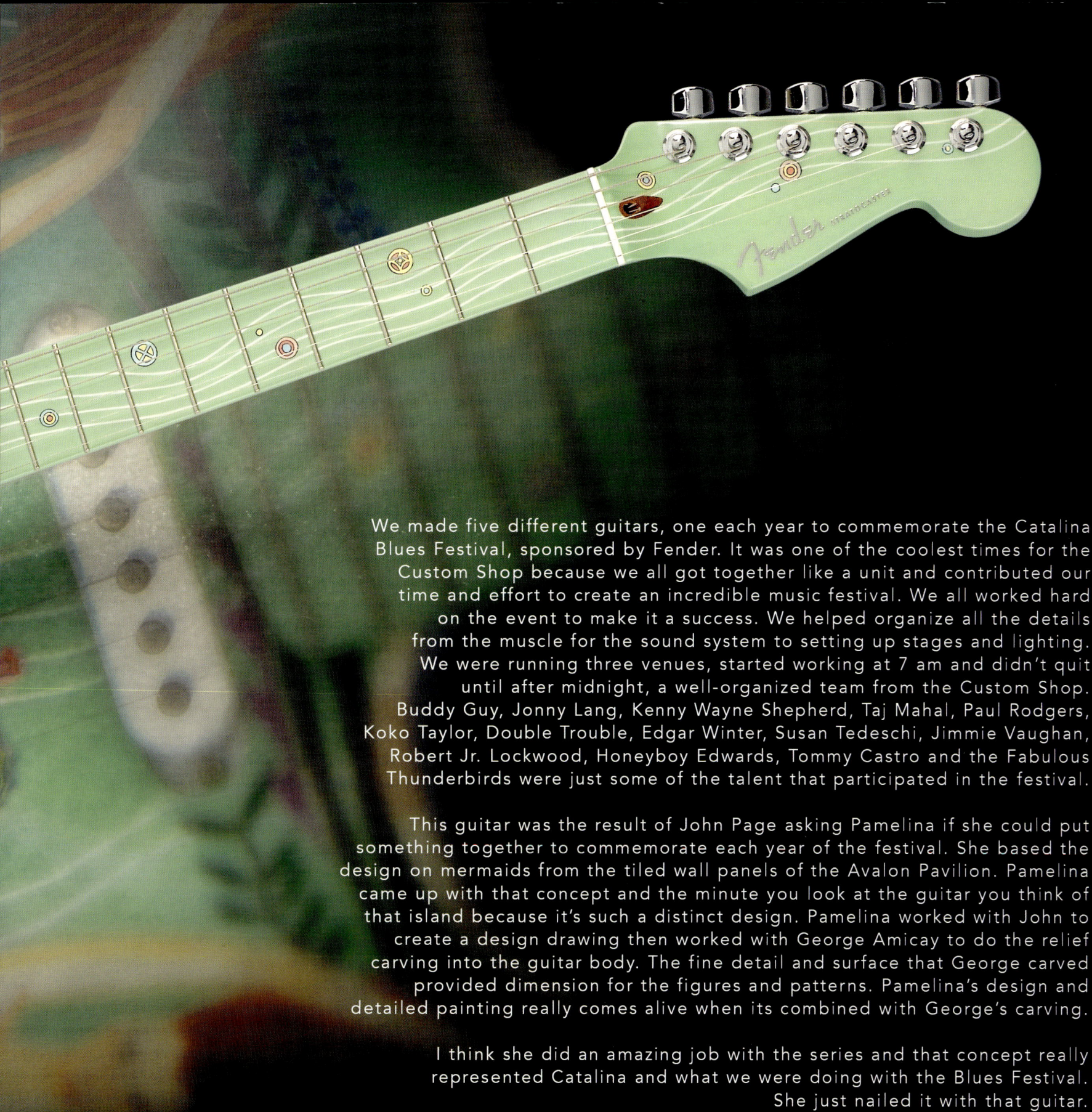

We made five different guitars, one each year to commemorate the Catalina Blues Festival, sponsored by Fender. It was one of the coolest times for the Custom Shop because we all got together like a unit and contributed our time and effort to create an incredible music festival. We all worked hard on the event to make it a success. We helped organize all the details from the muscle for the sound system to setting up stages and lighting. We were running three venues, started working at 7 am and didn't quit until after midnight, a well-organized team from the Custom Shop. Buddy Guy, Jonny Lang, Kenny Wayne Shepherd, Taj Mahal, Paul Rodgers, Koko Taylor, Double Trouble, Edgar Winter, Susan Tedeschi, Jimmie Vaughan, Robert Jr. Lockwood, Honeyboy Edwards, Tommy Castro and the Fabulous Thunderbirds were just some of the talent that participated in the festival.

This guitar was the result of John Page asking Pamelina if she could put something together to commemorate each year of the festival. She based the design on mermaids from the tiled wall panels of the Avalon Pavilion. Pamelina came up with that concept and the minute you look at the guitar you think of that island because it's such a distinct design. Pamelina worked with John to create a design drawing then worked with George Amicay to do the relief carving into the guitar body. The fine detail and surface that George carved provided dimension for the figures and patterns. Pamelina's design and detailed painting really comes alive when its combined with George's carving.

I think she did an amazing job with the series and that concept really represented Catalina and what we were doing with the Blues Festival. She just nailed it with that guitar.

Catalina Blues Festival Stratocaster® / 2001, Pamelina H.

"SkeleTele" Telecaster® / 2004, Master Builder, Chris Fleming

I had this idea of collaborating with local artists in the creation of art guitars and one of my artist friends, Dave Newman suggested I get in touch with Kit Carson to try some things with a guitar. Kit does a lot with skeletons and themes around the Day of the Dead celebration and I thought that would fit well with what we did in the Custom Shop. I sent Kit a Telecaster body to fool around with and he went into it with full force. Kit drew up the design in great detail then Ron Thorn did the inlays and Dan Lawrence did the airbrush painting according to Kit's original design. Kit did the engraving and silverwork set with precious stones like he does with his jewelry work.

At the time this set another benchmark for fantastic art guitars and it was the most expensive guitar yet to be produced by the Custom Shop. Yuriy has since shot that record to the moon and back. Topping it all off, this guitar sounded and played great, it wasn't all for decoration.

Chris Fleming, 2016

"Surfboard" Stratocaster® / 2004, Masterbuilder, Dennis Galuszka

All my life I've been studying old wooden surfboards and looking at anything related to them that I can find, I love those things. I built the first surf theme guitar in 1998 and after 18 years I still get three or four orders every year for these guitars. They just keep coming, which is great, I love it and yet I build them all a bit different from each other. I try to make each one with some unique feature so that they're all custom one-offs. This one's a little different because of the mix of woods and the tapered top lamination that we hadn't done before.

This one's a little different also because it's a 24" scale like a Jaguar and it has the Jaguar pick-ups, tremolo and bridge, so it's kind of a Jaguar in Strat clothing. The laminated woods on the top are great because when you put a top on a guitar it locks it together and makes it do it's thing with a little more ring and gives the guitar a little more sustain than usual.

Dennis Galuszka, 2016

"Surfboard" Stratocaster® / 2004, Masterbuilder, Dennis Galuszka

Stevie Ray Vaughan "Number One" Tribute Stratocaster® / 2004, Masterbuilder, John Cruz

When the opportunity came up to work on the SRV Number One, John English was originally going to do it but as sometimes happens, something came up and he was suddenly unavailable. We had a deadline and needed a prototype done so we could show Jimmie and the family. Mike Eldred came to me and asked if I was into doing this, I just grabbed for it and said for sure let's go, let's make it happen. This was the first big project I did as a masterbuilder with my master built decal on the back. The project almost put me in the ground because that guitar was so intense!

Mike brought in a box full of stuff related to the guitar, videotapes, photos and whatever they could find showing the guitar, I never got to see the actual guitar. I could only see images on a screen, magazines and photos. They had some pretty good video footage and I took that home to study. I would watch the video and actually stop it to measure the wear patterns, scratches and everything on the screen, then scaled the drawings and measurements up to actual size. That's how I came up with the specs for the prototype and when we sent it to Jimmie he pretty much loved it from the get go.

John Cruz, 2016

Burnishing electronics shielding / Masterbuilder, John Cruz, 2016

I started working at Fender in 1987 and I remember coming through on a tour before I was hired at the old factory where they had all the guitars overhead. There was a slue of fiesta red Strats. I don't know if they were 50's or 60s Strats but I saw that color and right away thought, that's a Gary Moore guitar, then another Gary Moore guitar, it was as if they were all over the place. That's when I knew I needed to get into this place, because I really wanted to be close to doing something like this. I did get the chance to do it along the way, working on several 50's 60's Strats and always thinking about Gary when I was working on them.

He played this guitar right up until he died. He was primarily known for playing the other brand guitars that we all know but he always took this one with him, even down to the blues stuff that he was pretty much always playing. So there's a whole story that goes on beyond this that's insanely memorable to me, it's killer to be a part of it.

John Cruz, 2016

"President George Washington" Custom Esquire® and amp set / 2004, Mike Eldred

The President George *(I cannot tell a lie)* Washington Cherry Esquire Custom is clean simple and right to the point. It was made from a fallen 100' cherry tree from my yard several years back during home construction. After saving and barn storing the wood for 10 years, I had it kiln dried and cut up into lumber, enough to build a complete bar, the guitar and amp set.

In this case, the George Washington axe, is the cherry tree. 12th fret inlayed *G. Washington*, Mike Eldred put the guitar and amp set together for me in 2004. The Fender Deluxe Custom Cherry Amp has nine Volume only controls. *That's not a lie.*

Rick Nielsen, 2016

Troy Lee Designs Stratocaster® / 2004, Masterbuilder, Todd Krause

Troy Lee was right down the street from us so we got right into it with those guys and we knew they would be perfect for guitars. This is typical of what you would see on racing helmets back then. They asked if they could do the neck as well, I thought that was so unique and cool. So we ended up doing what resembles a spine that goes up the back of the neck, I thought this whole thing was really cool.

Troy Lee started out painting helmets for motocross then went into all kinds of racing gear, motorcycles, cars and anything you can think of that moves fast. There's a crew of top-notch individuals, pin stripers, graphics guys, all the old school type of lettering and leafing techniques. These guys are definitely part of the SoCal custom culture.

Todd Krause, 2016

"El Cabron" / 2005, Masterbuilder, Chris Fleming

Fender's Custom Shop release of the special six-string 'lectric Spanish creation, "El Cabron", masterfully photo-documented by Steve Pitkin, stands as another shining example of the design expertise holding tradition from the vintage beginnings of Leo Fender who forged a worldly perception of simplicity-meets-electricity.

And, this one, too, carries yet another BFG stamp of approval. Thanks to Steve and the Fender Custom Shop for the views of beauty.

Billy F Gibbons, 2016

The Reverend Billy came to visit the shop one day with his famous box of Krispy Kreme's to share with everyone, he spent the day walking through the plant and digging in with us in the Custom Shop. He spotted me working on a one-piece Strat body with a hard-tail bridge and a neck with no truss-rod. He got real interested in what I was doing and asked what I thought of building a Strat body / Tele neck hybrid with a single bridge pick-up.

What's interesting is this guitar inspired the creation of the first Greasebucket® tone circuit that has since been installed in many guitars. I worked with Michael Frank-Braun to come up with a tone circuit that would work with just a single pick-up. We made a special noiseless pick-up that had a lot of output. Billy uses light .008 strings with the action set so low I didn't think I could build a Strat that would sound good and stay in tune with such light string tension. This guitar sounds great and is a standing testament to the Reverend's super light touch.

Chris Fleming, 2016

"El Cabron" / 2005, Masterbuilder, Chris Fleming

In this photo John is building a totally custom designed, Swingmaster Tele for Dan Smith, Jason Smith's dad. John believed the purpose of every guitar was to be played. He did build plenty of decorative art guitars but for John the true purpose of an instrument could not be superseded by artistic decoration.

So many people had so much talent in that place over the years but if I were to have any of them build me a guitar, it would have been John English. John did build very artistically appointed guitars but nothing that got in the way of it being a guitar, first.

Mark Kendrick, 2016

Sanding a neck joint / 1995, Masterbuilder, John English

Rosewood Neck Prototype Stratocaster / 2005, Masterbuilder, John English

John knew of an original guitar out there that would have been referred to as a prototype. It was a '56 or '57 Stratocaster with a one-piece rosewood neck. In 1999 John tried a mock-up of that guitar in desert sand with anodized gold guard and it was really nice. He was into trying to recreate some of the experimental prototypes of our past that never made it into full production. For John, the finishing details were his biggest focus, having a nice tight fit in the neck pocket, the back shape of a neck, fretwork, and every other element had to be right. His attention to detail was beyond anyone else in the shop.

You get a completely different sound out of a rosewood neck, it's not as bright sounding as a maple neck, but has a much darker and warmer sounding tone. On a 50's style Strat with an ash body it tends to darken out the tone and soften a lot of the highs. The anodized guard changes the inductive quality on the pick-ups so it does add back a little bit of higher tones but not the shrillness. I love this guitar, I thought it sounded great and had a nice warm tone.

Jason Smith, 2016

Rosewood Neck Prototype Stratocaster® / 2005, Masterbuilder, John English

"Buddy Guy" Custom Telecaster® / 2005, Masterbuilder, Yuriy Shishkov

This guitar was totally Buddy Guy's idea and I was the one who executed his design. He wanted a 70's type Telecaster with two Humbuckers, polka dots, blue pickguard and amplifier control knobs, like Muddy Waters. Obviously for Buddy Guy it had to be polka dots because that is his signature design, but blue for this guitar.

This guitar body is made from a single piece of ash, so light that when Buddy Guy received the guitar he thought we made a mistake and chambered the body, in truth it was one solid piece of very light weight ash. I know he loves this guitar because I see photos in magazines featuring him with this guitar. The Telecaster is a little special for him because he is so well known for playing a Stratocaster.

Yuriy Shishkov, 2016

"Buddy Guy" Custom Telecaster® / 2005, Masterbuilder, Yuriy Shishkov

Jeff Beck Tribute Esquire® / 2005, Masterbuilder, John Cruz

This was a 150 piece Limited Edition run of Jeff Beck's '54 Esquire. This guitar goes all the way back to the Yardbirds era with Jeff, he loved this Esquire so much but he wanted that feel of a Strat and not bothered about the collectability of the guitar, he took it to a local luthier who actually cut the body contours for him that were close to a Strat, not quite, but close. Jeff loved it and played it ever since and now it's cool to see early photos of it before he did the modification and then to look for later photos with the arm and belly contours cut in. I did the original prototype for Jeff and trained a group of guys and the builders to get the details right based on the proto that I had made. All of the sound came out of that single bridge pick-up so it became an obsession for us to get right.

It was a stock pick-up on a '54 Esquire. The vintage wiring was also stock, we have new wiring techniques to give you three or four different sounds with an Esquire but Jeff didn't use it. The single pick-up was the magic, one of the best sounding stock pick-ups I've heard. All the readings were taken from it and we tried to copy them perfectly and had the readings right where they should be but it didn't get the sound quite right.

Abby brought in a pick-up based out of her memory for pick-ups of the time. Looking back she could tell us which wire to use and the exact steps they followed to put it all together. She did it all the original way as it was done 40 years earlier and the sound match was insane. She could help us with the details because she was with Fender at that time. It was amazing to have her help to redesign that pick-up after 40 plus years.

John Cruz, 2016

"Master Salute" Limited Edition Stratocaster® / 2006, Masterbuilder, Mark Kendrick

The whole gold leaf concept started with Eric Clapton's yellow gold leaf guitar in 1996. After that, there were one or two but John English and I did a 20-piece run of yellow gold leaf guitars for Japan in 2003. Three years later Mike Eldred, as the Marketing Manager, requested this 250-piece run of white gold leaf guitars and called the series, *The Master Salute*. We did the run with all the masterbuilders at the time. The gold leafing was all hand applied, sheet after sheet and took hours to finish. We used white gold leaf instead of the yellow gold to make this run a bit different than what had been done previously.

Mark Kendrick, 2016

"Splattocaster" Stratocaster® / 2006, Masterbuilder, Scott Buehl

This all started with a design contest for Guitar World magazine. People were sending in little cartoons and descriptions of what they were dreaming of. This design was chosen. Our Director of Operations, Alex Nicholas came to me and said, "hey I have something right up your alley, this guy had designed a Strat with colored liquid windows, it's made out of aluminum." Perfect, I knew what to do, Alex chose me because I can work the metal on guitars like that. I made this one by hand, the entire thing. There's an esthetic that goes with the process of working through the steps in building a guitar that is as much a part of it as the finished instrument itself. It's all part of it, and that stuff happens with me in advance of doing the work. I think through the entire process including the assembly of a guitar way before it happens. I try to nail everything so that it's easy to put together. You can force things together and tighten them up gradually as you go along and it will kind of fit together or you can make it right and man, it just all goes together and fits like a glove.

I used to work at Jackson with Mike Shannon in the 80's. Mike would come over to my bench and ask if I knew how to sand a neck and I said yes of course, so then he said, "here sand these necks," then he would check the work and start marking it up with pencil marks, it was lumpy here, in just the right light you could see some scratches there. Those scratches would be gone as soon as the finish hit the wood, but Mike would not allow that stuff to go through. I was 18 when I started working with him, to this day I ask myself, would Mike Shannon let this go?

The apprenticeship teaching style is really the way to learn a high-level skill. As an apprentice, I thought I had achieved high standards but really I had achieved a little better than a production line standard, not even close to what Mike demanded. When you're a kid you really need a master's eye to guide your work until you get there on your own, I still know the day might come when Mike will look at one of my pieces and I wonder what he would say about the work.

Scott Buehl, 2016

Splattocaster™ Stratocaster® / 2006, Masterbuilder, Scott Buehl

"Blackie®" Tribute Stratocaster® / 2006, Masterbuilder, Todd Krause

This project was long anticipated, it seemed whenever I did an interview I was asked, when are you going to do Blackie and 2006 was the year. Guitar Center commissioned the build after they bought it at auction, putting it into high gear.

There was a big media release. Guitar Center built it up and leaked what was being done, the big banner across the street on Sunset Blvd, over Sam Ash and the whole thing. There were less than 200 pieces made and they sold all of them in 20 minutes, which for GC was a great "Blackie Friday" release. It was not an easy project, even though a lot of the techniques I needed had already been developed on earlier projects, this had to be a perfect copy of Blackie. It's not like you get to do a neck and if it doesn't look quite right say, *close enough*.

It was intimidating at first studying, how was I going do this? There was not typical fingerboard wear on this neck. I was able to come up with some techniques that worked very well. The neck had been stripped, resanded, refretted and refinished, which is why it was undersize. The paint job had not worn like a typical Fender. There was earlier wear underneath the refinish and what I thought looked like whiskers on the back of the neck. I was able to come up with a way to get that effect in the right areas before it went into paint so that when the guitar was reliced we would get that multi-layer relic finish that matched the original.

The pick-ups had been modified. They have copper shielding around the coils that is grounded, what I call a classic rock hot-rod, an early form of a noiseless pick-up, and a common 70's modification. It wasn't perfect but it helped shield the 60-cycle hum and it does give the pick-up a certain kind of sound. To this day, still one of my favorite mods to my personal guitars.

Todd Krause, 2016

Original mojo makers / 2007, Abigail Ybarra and George Fullerton

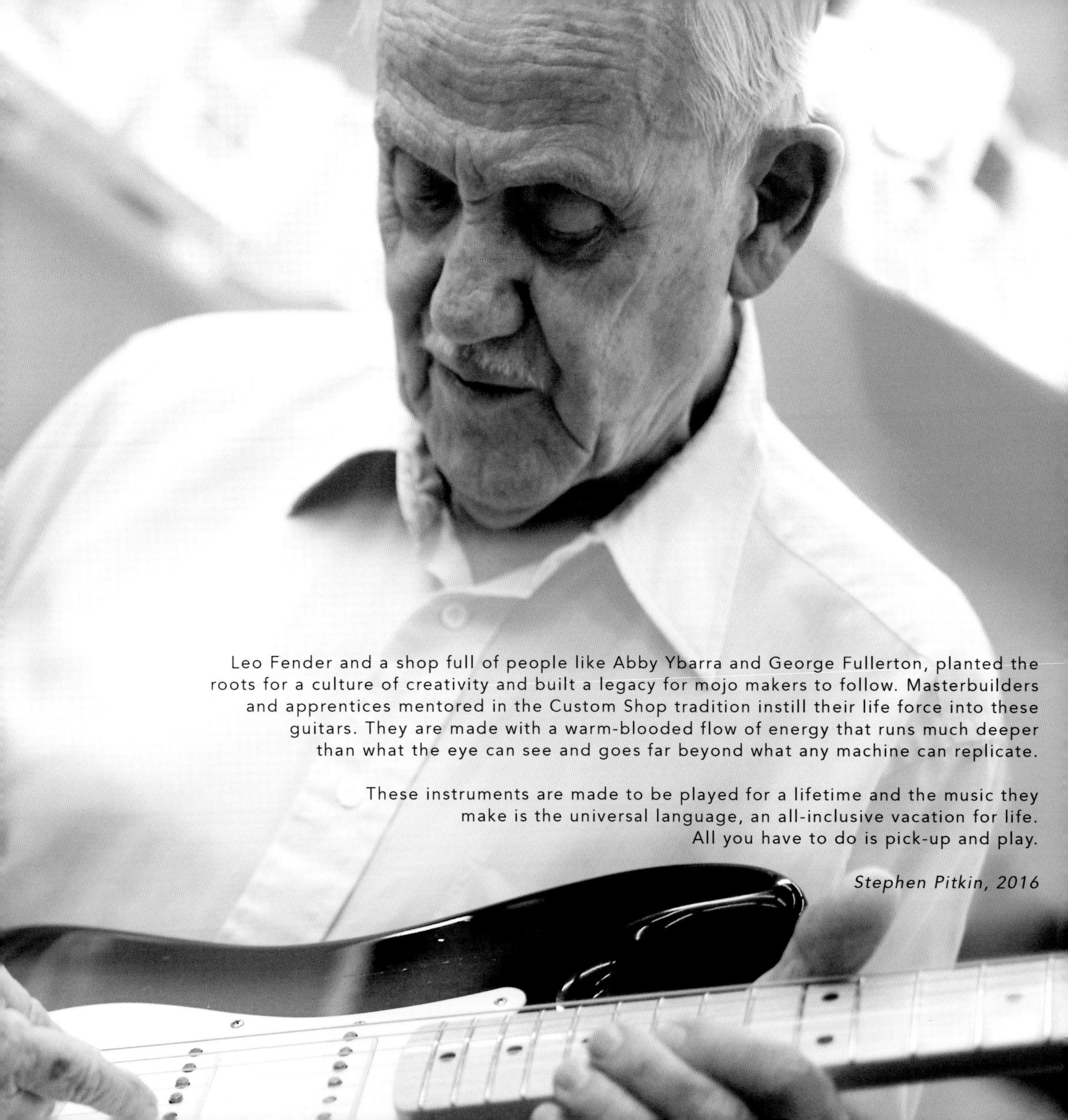

Leo Fender and a shop full of people like Abby Ybarra and George Fullerton, planted the roots for a culture of creativity and built a legacy for mojo makers to follow. Masterbuilders and apprentices mentored in the Custom Shop tradition instill their life force into these guitars. They are made with a warm-blooded flow of energy that runs much deeper than what the eye can see and goes far beyond what any machine can replicate.

These instruments are made to be played for a lifetime and the music they make is the universal language, an all-inclusive vacation for life. All you have to do is pick-up and play.

Stephen Pitkin, 2016

Custom Stratocaster® / 2007, Masterbuilder, Jason Smith

We had a dealer event coming up and I wanted to do something that would stand out on the rack. It was at a time before we built the San Dimas type guitars and there was a demand building up for them. I thought the reverse peg-head would lend itself well to the attitude I was going for, driving home the hard rock kind of vibe.

I was going for a cross between a Fender and a Charvel. Guys really wanted a two pick-up hot-rod Strat so I built something to meet that demand. This guitar had a hard tail American Standard steel bridge with stainless steel saddles. The switching was five-way, with only two pick-ups; full hum, split hum, full hum and neck, split hum and neck, and the neck by itself so you had an array of tones out of two pick-ups. The neck had a flat 12" radius with medium jumbo frets, pretty much everything required to make a real shredder guitar. The skull and crossbones were applied with layers of silver leaf. I drew and cut the masking template by hand to keep it a bit rough. We finished the entire guitar with a flat satin black finish.

Jason Smith, 2016

Custom Stratocaster® / 2007, Masterbuilder, Jason Smith

"KoiCaster" Stratocaster® / 2008, Masterbuilder, Todd Krause

The big challenge with graphics and inlays on a guitar has always been how to get artwork gracefully to wrap around the edges and onto the back and neck. That problem really got me thinking, how can I engineer a way to weave the artwork into the guitar. One way to do it is to tie the neck into the body with the design. With this guitar, fish are swimming down the neck into the pond, when you do something like this you tie the whole composition together, it's smooth and complete, top to bottom.

Ron Thorn came in and we talked for a while and this was a concept I had in mind except originally I had it reversed, in and talking to Ron, we had one of those *ah-ha* moments. I would say it was at least four or five years in the incubation process just that same question coming up over and over again.

Fish swimming down the neck makes the composition smooth and complete, top to bottom. That's the easy part, It also appears like the deck wraps around the body, which is a simple enough idea but everybody who studies it carefully kind of has a brain freeze, trying to figure out how we did it. Ron Thorn did the inlays and Dan Lawrence painted the shadows and edging to give it more of a 3D effect, and of course that flame maple that I like to use always reminds me of a cool running stream.

Todd Krause, 2016

"KoiCaster" Stratocaster® / 2008, Masterbuilder, Todd Krause

Jazzmaster™ Bass VI Doubleneck / 2010, Masterbuilder, Dennis Galuszka

This just had to be done.
The inspiration for this was simply my love for offset guitars and I really wanted to mash these two guitar types together. I found a single piece of ash that was big enough for a one-piece body. I've always loved offset guitars and chrome, which is why I went with the Jaguar plate on the Jazzmaster type guitar. I like seeing the contrast between wood, plastic and chrome, I think it looks nice.

The reason I left the center pick-up out on the Bass VI neck was so I could use the stock plate for the Bass VI so the switches are just on-off for each pick-up, four switches for four pick-ups. That switching set up allowed me to keep everything on one circuit. The volume and tone work for the whole guitar and I thought would be a lot simpler with that set up.

Dennis Galuszka, 2016

Pre-cutting the nut / 1999, Masterbuilder, Dennis Galuszka

This is the initial slotting of the nut, setting the string spacing, angles and general depth in a step we call pre-cutting the nut. It is one of of first steps in setting up a nearly finished guitar.

This step is extremely important in setting the spacing and the angle of the string from the nut to the post and the nut to frets. You don't want the angle too much or too little and then of course the depth of the nut has to be right.

If it's too high that F chord is a nightmare to grab and it's going to throw off your intonation. If it's too low you will get string buzz. When you've done a few thousand of these it becomes second nature, but that is what it takes. Everything is easy when practiced a few thousand times but it's one of those things that you can definitely tell when it's done well or not.

Dennis Galuszka, 2016

"Dave Newman" Telecaster® / 2011, Masterbuilder, Greg Fessler

I collect old relics and mementos that I find on our travels thru the Southwest and incorporate them into each guitar. These items carry a sort of memory of their past experiences. We recognize some of them as references to our own past. The worn components hint of treasured memories that when combined trigger a new creative expression that is imagined a little differently for everyone and yet feels very personal. The time and thought that goes into the design, balance and juxtaposition of the elements is part of the creative process that I build into each composition.

Dave Newman, 2016

Dave Newman takes a lot of time and thought in what he's trying to do, he has an idea in his head of what he's trying to accomplish and what he's trying to bring out. Some of his themes are Western art others are Googie art, he does change it up a bit to go with what he feels inspired by, depending what he has to work with or what he has collected at the time. I think he's really connected to the past and Fender guitars are a 50's design, so Dave's artwork ties right in.

Greg Fessler, 2016

"Dave Newman" Telecaster® / 2011, Masterbuilder, Greg Fessler

"Birdflower" Telecaster® / 2011, Masterbuilder, Yuriy Shishkov

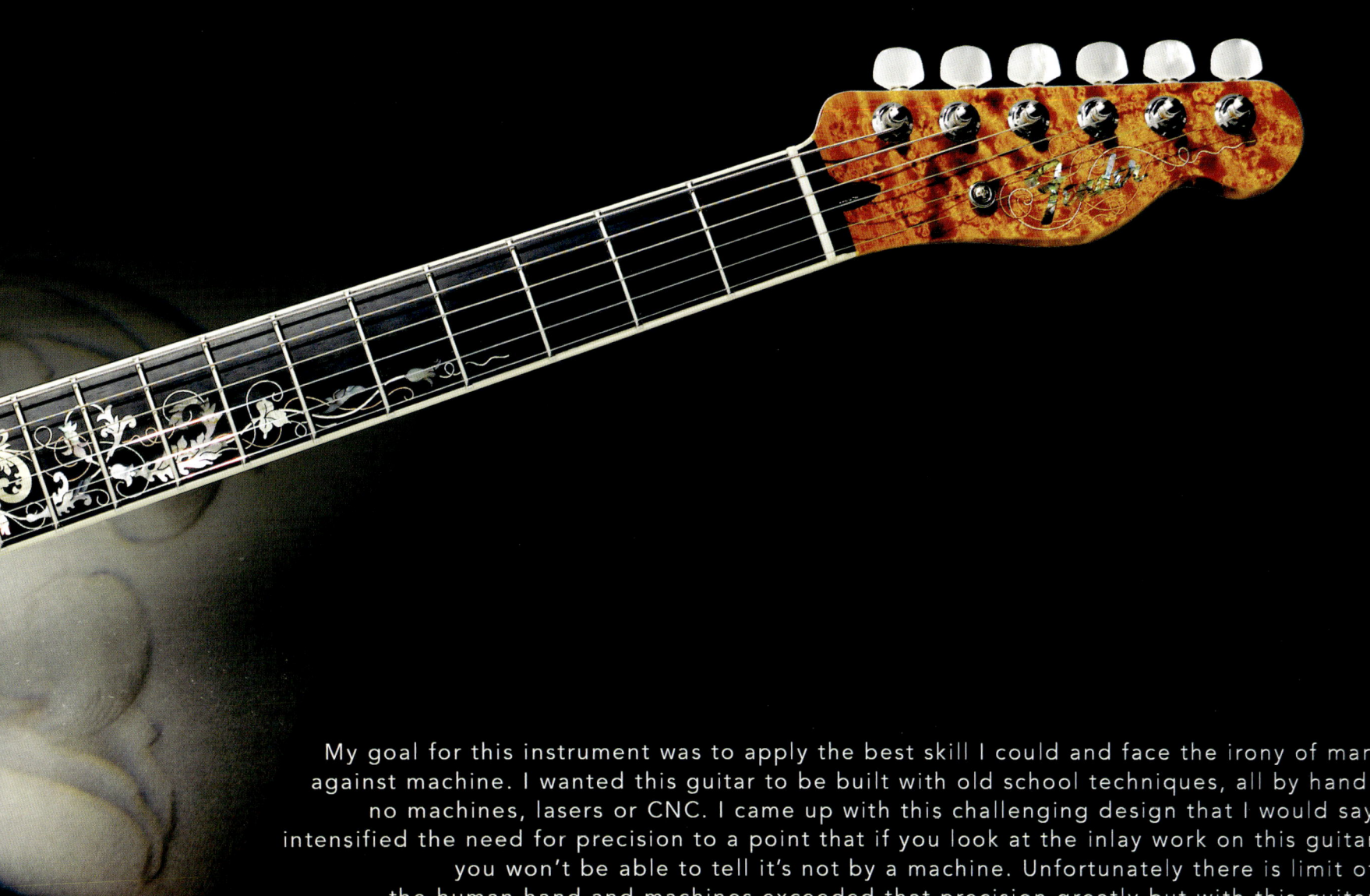

My goal for this instrument was to apply the best skill I could and face the irony of man against machine. I wanted this guitar to be built with old school techniques, all by hand, no machines, lasers or CNC. I came up with this challenging design that I would say intensified the need for precision to a point that if you look at the inlay work on this guitar you won't be able to tell it's not by a machine. Unfortunately there is limit of the human hand and machines exceeded that precision greatly but with this guitar I tried to surpass the quality of a machine.

I tried to create something in the design that no machine could do. For example, if you make the tip of a leaf that comes to a sharp point, you can cut the pieces on a machine with no problem. However, if you use a machine to cut the pocket the cutter will make the edges round, not sharp. I can still cut that perfect point by hand with a chisel and finish with a sharp knife, making the point of the leaf absolutely sharp. The sharp point of an inlay piece then fits inside the pocket. There is a real benefit to working by hand. It is kind of strange that we have to mimic machines these days but that's almost what I was trying to do.

The material was clear walnut top and back over an ash body, ebony fingerboard, abalone and mother of pearl inlays and inlayed silver wire. The hardware was hand engraved by Tim Adlam, an amazing custom engraver, it would have been a crime to do the engraving on a machine.

Yuriy Shishkov, 2016

"Birdflower" Telecaster® / 2011, Masterbuilder, Yuriy Shishkov

"Sparkle Flame" Stratocaster® / 2012, Masterbuilder, Dennis Galuszka

There is a fire theme burning in the graphics and I wanted this entire guitar to reflect that attitude as well, so this became a hot-rod guitar through and through. Jay Nelson painted the red sparkle flames here at Fender and he made them to fade out as they move up the body of the guitar, emulating a flame getting less intense as it rises.

The guitar is set up with a custom two-point tremolo system, LSR roller nut, locking tuners and fueled by extra hot pick-ups. It is intended to be a true hot-rod that you might beat up on more than usual when you play it and this guitar is really made to scream.

Dennis Galuszka, 2016

"Liberty" Stratocaster® / 2013, Masterbuilder, Dale Wilson

This guitar is totally American, what about the Stratocaster isn't innovative and revolutionary? I like the flow of the design with the shape of the body and the historical theme of it. It's not what I would think of as the typical Stratocaster hot-rod theme, but it certainly has that same spirit in a different way.

I had worked with Frank Germano previously and I asked him if he had any ideas that would fit a guitar. He was working with a *Colonial Liberty* theme so I asked him to sketch out some ideas that might work on a Strat. We worked together on the design fitting around the contours of the body. I wanted it to be a light relic so that it looked like an old piece of paper or historic document. Altogether, I think Ben Franklin would have loved this guitar.

Dale Wilson, 2016

"Rascal" Bass / 2013, Masterbuilder, Jason Smith

I wanted to make a short scale bass that didn't feel awkward like most short scale basses. It is set up with light gauge strings, narrower spacing from string to string, smaller neck, smaller nut width, overall a comfortable bass for smaller hands. The major issue I've always had with any short scale bass is they never seem to balance well on the strap, they usually don't sound that great and they're hard to play. You're constantly battling how to hold the neck up. This is a 30" scale but the horn comes up all the way to where it's parallel to the 13th fret. The guitar balances better on the strap because of where the neck is set. I don't recall us ever doing anything like this at Fender.

Shorter scale length is a benefit for a smaller person or someone just starting out playing. I received a letter from a Nashville session guy who really likes this bass because he has tendonitis in his elbow and wrist and has a hard time playing a standard size bass. This actually helps him a lot, it hangs and feels like a standard bass but is much easier to play.

I wanted to incorporate a lot of the 70's stuff into this bass, that's the stuff I grew up with, lipstick pick-ups, offset bodies, pearloid guards and all. It's actually the body perimeter of a Bass VI, the neck is a Coronado bass neck and I changed the orientation of the face dots and used different tuning keys. The bridge is a Starfire bridge from a Guild, I just took a bunch of different things we had available and rearranged them in a new way.

Jason Smith, 2016

"Rascal" Bass / 2013, Masterbuilder, Jason Smith

Checking the bow of a bass neck / 2016, Masterbuilder Jason Smith

Before I started apprenticing with John English, I had already been working in various departments of the Custom Shop for a good 10 to 12 years. I had a basic skill set but through my apprenticeship with John, I refined those skills to get to where I'm at now. He taught me to pay attention and focus on all the fine details. It was very important to him that I actually learn the history of all of the Fender products, the differences that developed over the years, when they changed certain screws and parts and woods and everything else. That was how I was taught over 17 years of practice.

John was really good at pushing to get a higher quality level of work out of me. If I did something that wasn't up to his standard it didn't go through and he would push and push until I could do things exactly as he expected them done. With that type of training I was able to fine-tune a lot of my skills, the way I look at guitars and how I approach building guitars.

Jason Smith, 2016

Carved Top Telecaster® / 2014, Masterbuilder, Paul Waller

I saw the Custom Shop missing something in the realm of classic hollow-body guitars and built the carved-top Telecaster to fill the missing space for Fender. This guitar is built with a carved flame maple top, a semi-hollow ash body and is finished with double binding and double f-holes. The neck is also bound and the ebony fingerboard is set with pearl *thumbnail* fret markers adding to the 50's vibe.

The body structure is a solid ash block whittled away, opening it all up inside. Basically, everything is hollow except for a couple blocks supporting the pick-ups and the bridge. When you strum it without it plugged in you can hear the acoustic qualities of it really well. It's much louder than a Tele Thin-line. I call the color burnt orange. It is Tennessee orange thinned out quite a bit to get a softer mellow color, I did not like the overcooked tea look so typical on guitars of this type. The binding and the gold hardware add a classy touch to the finish of the guitar.

Paul Waller, 2016

Carved Top Telecaster® / 2014, Masterbuilder, Paul Waller

Hermitage Stratocaster / 2014, Masterbuilder, Yuriy Shishkov

The idea behind this guitar was the 250 year anniversary of the Hermitage State Museum Palace in St. Petersburg, Russia. Everybody in Russia knows what the Hermitage is and it is special to me because that's where my roots are from. I was born in St. Petersburg and the Hermitage represents the most incredible collections of art in the world. From the beauty of the architecture to the art pieces and fine crafted objects in the collection, you name it. It's something I wanted to build in a guitar because so many aspects of this place are really close to me.

Claro walnut has the warmth of antique furniture. If you go through the Hermitage and look at the furniture you'll find similarities in color and material as well as finish. I used the hand-applied varnish and you can see on the instrument that it has a really gentle shine, similar to the old furniture. It is an extremely intense and complex process to apply.

This guitar has 75 feet of 18-karat gold wire inlayed by hand. It is set with more than 1,000 individually handset gemstones, 556 diamonds, 281 emeralds, 100 rubies and 70 sapphires. The hand-engraved control knobs and pick-up covers are all plated in 23 carat gold.

Yuriy Shishkov, 2016

Hermitage Stratocaster® / 2014, Masterbuilder, Yuriy Shishkov

"Sunset" quilted maple Stratocaster® / 2014, Built by Masterbuilder, Paul Waller

I was inspired to build this guitar while watching the Southern California sunset at the beach. The color was hand stained, mixed and rubbed on the surface of the wood until I got the blue to green burst the way I wanted. I mixed orange into the center, but wanted just a bit for the sunset to come through and meet the water. The figured wood and mix of color got the effect I was looking for.

We have the most outstanding materials available to work with. It's insane when you get stuff like this in your hands, take it into the light and watch the figured textures in the wood reflect light at different angles, it's really impressive, even before the wood is finished.

Paul Waller, 2016

Mastodon™ Bass VI / 2013, Masterbuilder: Dennis Galuszka

The neck inlays are Mastodon ivory and I nicknamed the guitar, *The Mastodon*. The neck pick-up is a Curtis Novak gold foil, a vintage style pick-up that he brought back to life. It's very thin and it still puts out almost 11k, a really high output so we had to match the bridge pick-up to keep up with it, but it really helped with the output, especially with the deeper tones.

This guitar has a Bass VI neck but it functions more as a baritone than a true Bass VI. I set it up to use baritone strings, which are smaller so you can play more guitar-style music with it.
I love that everybody who played it couldn't put it down.

Dennis Galuszka, 2016

"Mastodon" Bass VI / 2015, Masterbuilder, Dennis Galuszka

Sanding fretboard roll / 2016, Masterbuilder, Dennis Galuszka

This is the step in making a neck we call a fretboard roll. If you don't bevel back the board edge into itself, the frets cantilever over the round of the fingerboard making it really uncomfortable to play. If you round the fretboard edge back a little bit it all becomes one with the neck and the edges of the frets.

The sander is cutting an angle, enabling us to round off, then later we will manually finish softening the fingerboard and fret edges in fine detail. Without a bevel the fret will feel like it's hanging over the round edge of the fretboard. This all helps the frets become part of the round edge instead of hanging over the edge, making the guitar much more comfortable to play.

Dennis Galuszka, 2016

Custom Precision Bass® / 2015, Masterbuilder, Greg Fessler

On a trip to Japan in 2008, I visited 40 to 50 guitar shops with one memorable shop specializing in boutique basses, the place was full of beautifully crafted custom basses but they had no Fenders. The shop owner challenged me to make a boutique style Fender bass and I took the challenge. The word boutique means something special, and with a bass that means killer wood, abalone, special binding and hardware. Just about every specialty detail I could think of went into this bass, right down to the gold hardware.

Maple necks definitely have a lot to do with the sound of a guitar, more so than the body. One of the greatest aspects of tone in a guitar is definitely the wood of the neck. Flame grained wood is a little softer and not as bright sounding as quarter sawn wood. The direction of the grain and the weight of the wood also have a big affect on the tone of a guitar.

Greg Fessler, 2016

"Jawbreaker" Stratocaster® / 2016, Masterbuilder, Dale Wilson

The Jawbreaker Strat was a collaboration between our own Custom Shop painter Jay Nelson and myself and was inspired by what jewelry auto workers would make out of huge paint chips that built up over time in the factory. We made this with right around 21 layers of paint built up over the top of each other then sanded through. The more I worked it I could see the contrasting colors revealed from top to bottom.

It reminds me of the Jawbreaker candy we would get as a child. What I loved about working on it was watching the colors pop out through the process of working. I was trying to get as much variety as possible without burning it or going through layers to the wood. I worked with an orbital sander all the way down to 1200 grit and threw some clear finish over it to bring out the depth and contrast of the colors.

Every detail of this guitar needed to be amazing from the figured maple neck to the crazy variety of color. This guitar was built for fun and made to be played.

Dale Wilson, 2016

"Jawbreaker" Stratocaster® / 2016, Masterbuilder, Dale Wilson

Profiling a nut / 2016, Masterbuilder Dale Wilson

Profiling the nut by hand is not hard but doing it correctly and doing it so it feels really good and plays right is something that's only won over time. It's a very important procedure in the functionality of the guitar. We're cutting it down to spec to the correct height so it will receive the strings without the strings going too deep or too shallow. Rounding and shaping the nut correctly makes it feel smooth at the end of the fret board, so it is as comfortable as the rest of the neck.

Dale Wilson, 2016

"Stained Glass" Telecaster / 2016, Masterbuilder, Dale Wilson

The stained glass Telecaster was inspired by the artwork of Annahita Hessami who created stained glass Telecaster panels for a guitar store in the UK which got me thinking, rather than a window we might try an actual stained glass guitar. I imagined a Van Gogh type starry night sky and moon light. I found Judson Studios nearby in Los Angeles, they were game to try it and started throwing sketches at me. This design worked really well. We made two bodies, one for them to fit and the other for me to make as a finished guitar.

We found thin light panels with LED's mounted only around the rim. The light travels through grooves cut across the panel, that way it's not a bunch of little hot-spot dots behind the glass. What's great about this art guitar is that it is not just locked up in a cabinet out of sight. John 5 is actually playing the guitar lit on stage, I have seen photos and it looks amazing on the big screen.

Dale WIlson, 2016

"Cardboard" Stratocaster® / 2016, Masterbuilder, Paul Waller

I had been over at Signal Snowboards, a handmade snowboard company in Huntington Beach experimenting with tweed snowboards and having some fun with odd materials. They put me in touch with Ernest Packaging who made snowboards, skateboards and bicycles with corrugated cardboard. They wanted to try a guitar and I said yea, let's go for it. Cardboard is about as far out there as we could ever imagine for a material that would work for a guitar but it stirred up and helped to clarify a few questions about what matters most in the tone of an electric guitar.

I have always believed the most important factors affecting the tone of an electric guitar are the neck, the bridge and the pick-ups. The rest of the tone woods add a lot of color and seasoning but are secondary in priority. This experiment seems to back that up because the cardboard guitar really does sound like a Stratocaster. Certainly not with the full voice of a Custom Shop instrument built with quality tone woods but it does sound like a Strat. It really drives home why we use maple for necks. Maple is the best tone wood on the planet. We've made necks out of everything else and we always go back to maple. This guitar has set a benchmark for how important wood is in the role of a guitar's tone.

Paul Waller, 2016

Rosewood Flame Maple Stratocaster® / 2016, Masterbuilder, Greg Fessler

I have never seen a guitar built like this before. I've always loved figured woods and thought about doing something special with maple combined with rosewood. My first thought was the flame maple top on a rosewood guitar, then Ralph Esposito suggested making a flame wood pickguard as well. I made this pickguard from the same slab of wood that I used for the top and it's almost crazy how closely the grain lined up. I was able to get it to match so that even after all the cutting and sanding to spec, the parts came together and looked like one piece of maple.

Our rosewood guitars are chambered because rosewood is heavy and you try to lighten them up as much as possible. I do a lot of guitars with alder or ash bodies with rosewood necks and it seems to be super popular. People like them because you don't get the heaviness of the rosewood body but you still get some of that rosewood sound through the neck. The maple top is a good combination with the rosewood neck for the sound of the guitar, you get the warm rosewood aspect of the tone brightened up a bit with the maple top.

Greg Fessler, 2016

Rosewood Flame Maple Stratocaster® / 2016, Masterbuilder, Greg Fessler

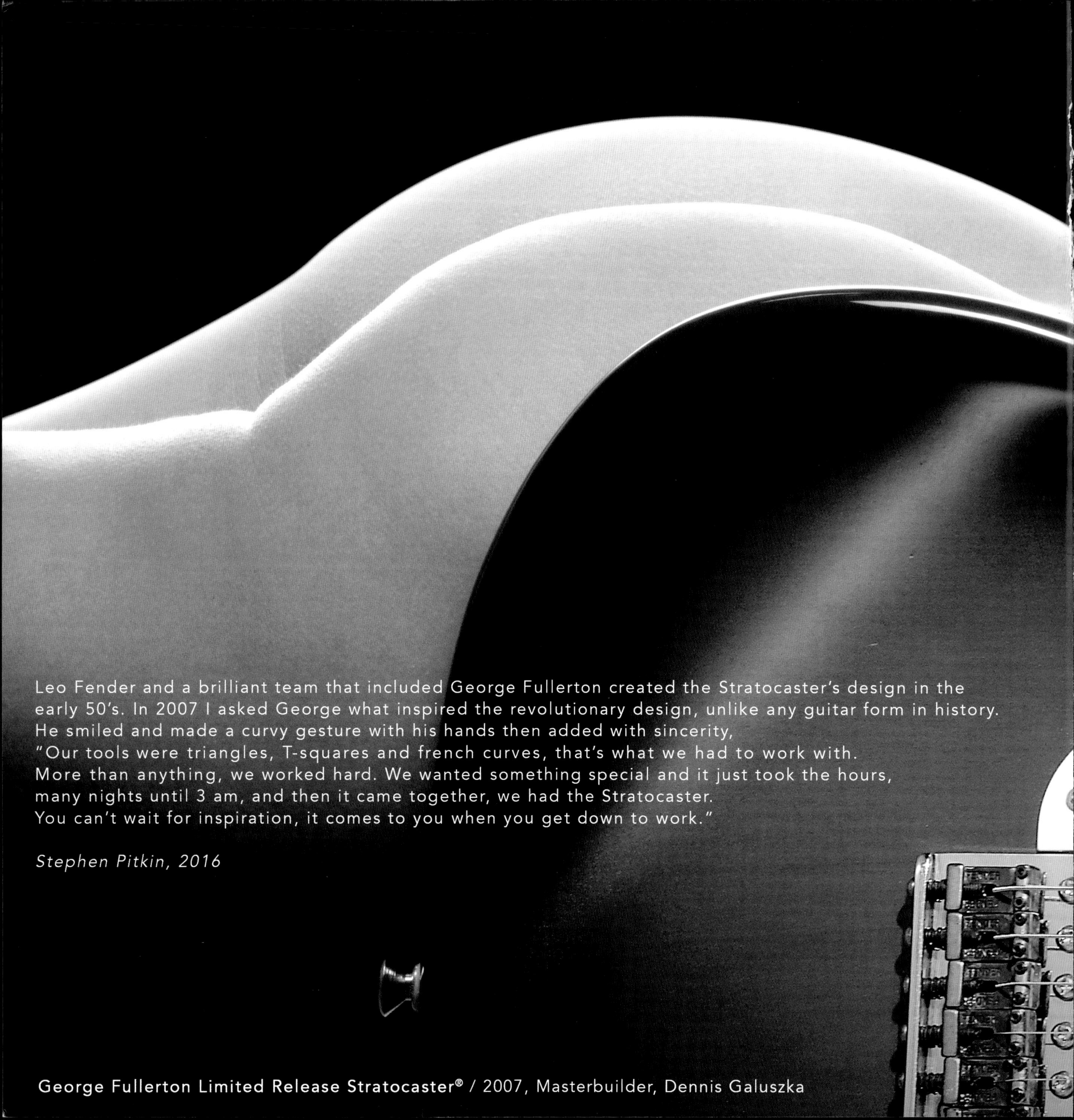

Leo Fender and a brilliant team that included George Fullerton created the Stratocaster's design in the early 50's. In 2007 I asked George what inspired the revolutionary design, unlike any guitar form in history. He smiled and made a curvy gesture with his hands then added with sincerity,
"Our tools were triangles, T-squares and french curves, that's what we had to work with.
More than anything, we worked hard. We wanted something special and it just took the hours, many nights until 3 am, and then it came together, we had the Stratocaster.
You can't wait for inspiration, it comes to you when you get down to work."

Stephen Pitkin, 2016

George Fullerton Limited Release Stratocaster® / 2007, Masterbuilder, Dennis Galuszka

Thank You **John Cerullo, Brad Smith** and Hal Leonard,

for finding merit in the publication of this book.

Thank You **Mike Lewis** and the Fender Custom Shop,

for sharing the vision in this project and helping bring it all together.

Thank You **Billy Gibbons,**

for the inspiration, the music and all things, El Cabron.

Thank You **Susan Pitkin,**

for your never-ending encouragement and support in all we do.

Stephen Pitkin